THE UNDERMINING OF THE DEMOCRATIC CLUB

ROB COOK

SPUYTEN DUYVIL   *New York City*

ACKNOWLEDGEMENTS

Arsenic Lobster: After Russia, In the Lights of the Church-Town Earth
The Bitter Oleander: The Sniper's Apartment, After America (VI), The Dawn
Animals, Presidents Day, My Friend The Death Legislator, After America (III)
Caliban: The Undermining of the Democratic Club
The Canary: Countries Between My Closet and the Subway
Cutthroat: Presidents Day
Fence: The Song of America, Notes from the Atrocities of the Land
Fissure: The Dirtbag On Election Day
Hampden-Sydney Poetry Review: Headline Song
Massachusetts Review: Campaign Speech
Mudfish: The President I Love, The Song Of Iraq, Human Flowers
Oranges & Sardines: Fascist Silence and a Sepia Democracy
Paterson Literary Review: Articulate Ferns
Poetry International: Countries Between My Closet and the Subway
Pleiades: Terror Song (II)
Quiddity: In Afghanistan
Rainbow Curve: In The Lights Of The Church-Town Earth
Tampa Review: Fascist Silence and a Sepia Democracy
Tarpaulin Sky: Stone Snow After You Wandered
Terminus: The Dawn Animals
Third Coast: The Sniper's Apartment
Tiferet: After America
Ur Vox: At The Ends Of My Country, Border Person,
          In the Absence of Great Men
The Yalobusha Review: Campaign Speech
"The Song of America" was reprinted in Best American Poetry 2009, guest editor
David Wagoner.

Library of Congress Cataloging-in-Publication Data

Cook, Rob, 1969-
 [Poems. Selections]
 The undermining of the Democratic Club : poems / by Rob Cook.
   pages ; cm
 ISBN 978-1-941550-17-5 (alk. paper)
 I. Title.
 PS3603.O5756A6 2015
 811'.6--dc23

                    2014023398

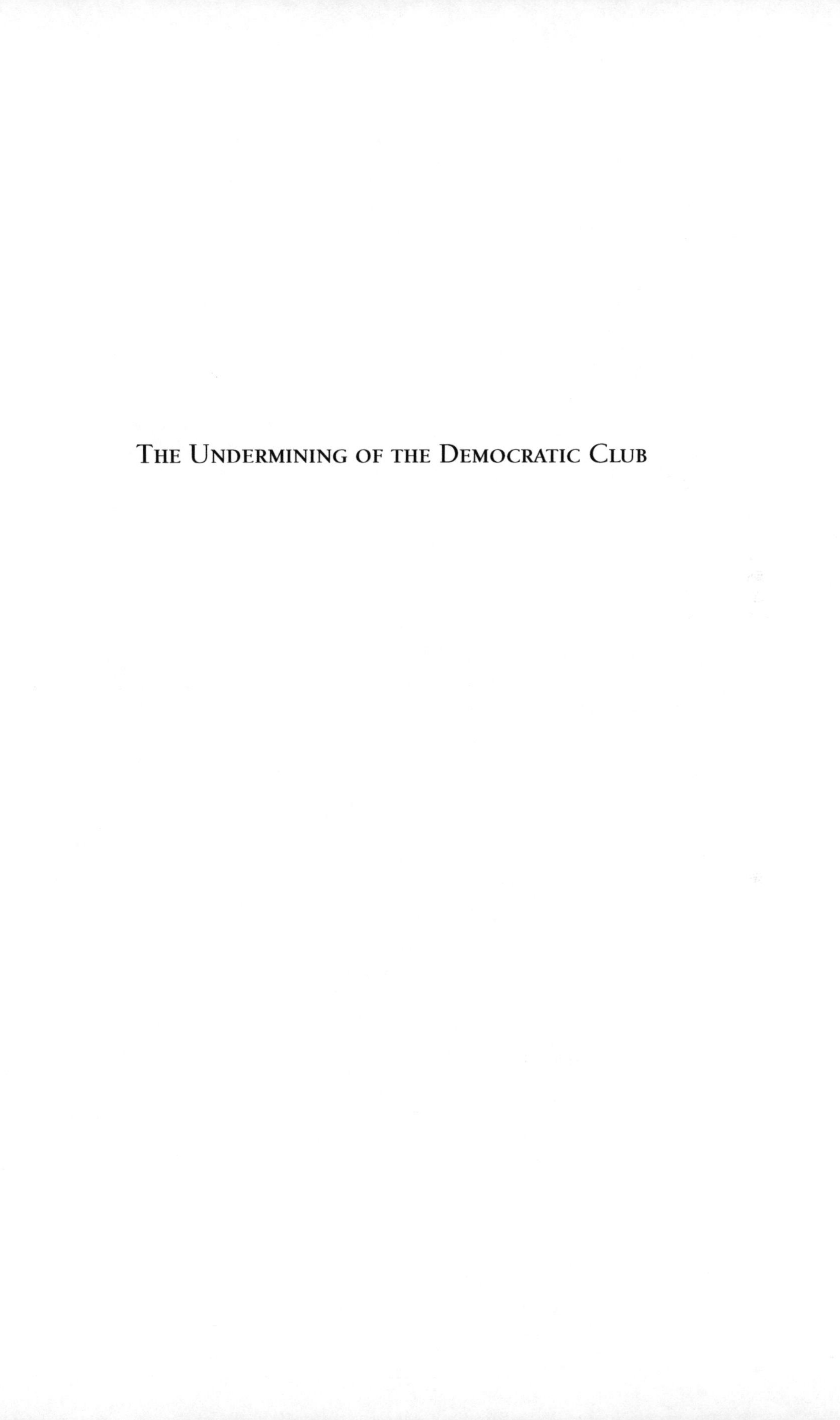

The Undermining of the Democratic Club

GOD BLESS AMERICA

is it worse to kill a woman or the clothes made of tongues
   that belong to the woman.
is it worse to eat a very stupid man or a tree that destroys oxygen.
is it worse to burn empty ice cream containers
or decapitate the person at your job
who dies three times from toe cancer
and comes back concerned about famine cults
and the faking of their obscurity.
is it worse to murder a dime or an ex-senator from connecticut.
a stick of chewing gum or the CEO of a masturbation blog.
is it worse to murder tarantulas, mafia men, serial killers
than it is to bludgeon your daughter's dance friend,
the family next door in that other universe,
broadcast by tribes of acne
a hundred miles into the dying bathroom mirror.
everybody knows about their own suffering.
nobody is clean, not your houseplants,
not the boy with the red flannel coat who rides his bike
past your house every morning at seven.
even the clouds are assassins.
even the mountains arranged in diamondback patterns
lurching across an earthquake map
assigned by the only president to ever kill himself.
what can be said about those who still think
of america as a place of healing,
those who still lie about unspeakable things.
even childrens' dolls tossed in the trash
touch at least once by accident.

PART ONE

Darkening Dust Village to the North

WE WELCOME ALL.
(only a stone's memory
of crawling toward dust villages
allowed beyond the border crossing,
a heat line on the map of an illegal's
determined but thirst-strangled body.)

Who could trust
the flag with its middle finger
aimed at Mexico, Pakistan, Iraq?

WE WELCOME ALL.

Here is your handful of water.
Here is your heritage of names
killed off with our landlines.
Here is a ceiling stain
that resembles a los angeles
claimed by no one.

WE WELCOME ALL.

The snakes will bring you their jails at night,

their coliseums of electrical storms
where no language is spoken.

WE WELCOME ALL
WHO'VE LOST THEIR WAY TO MORNING.

The flag, when it gives up its shivering cities,
can be rolled into a ball of blood.

"Who will companion the barren, widowed curtains?"
the house groans, a mild perversion.

A man brings a knife to bed.

By tomorrow he'll have gutted
the infant suicide choirs
inhabiting his sleep.

The same man who sits down to pee.

WE WELCOME ALL THAT STAY SILENT.

You will have to learn our incomplete words.
You will have to forget
every previous thing by heart.
You will have to add one hour to every day.

You will have to subtract ten mountains
and ten skies and ten underground oceans from your name.

If your facial kindness does not wilt on camera, we welcome you.
If you work for free, we welcome you.
If you hate the chelation therapists and the green mountain past
and all healing forms of sleep, we welcome you.

WE WELCOME ALL WHO SHARE
THE GOALS OF OUR STARS AND STRIPES.

All skulls. All skulls and fake water mentioned by no one.

Hussein's body bleeding from the sky's penitentiary
mentioned by no one.

But it's pretty.

We have such pretty ways to destroy where we're standing.

The flag loses its direction
like our bones lose their way in us.

Between Each of the Father's Rooms

The arguments of couch suicides next door
settle into the wall, the only thought
separating furniture they're hiding

and the stillness I've disturbed with my prayers,

the dark, blood-raw television
preaching the war between each
of God's rooms.

In one the windows have turned
to red paint, and in the kitchen our whispers
can no longer hold us on their backs,
and in one closet a fetus
suckles its own wet brimstone.

Many here in the middle of the darkness of heaven
have rusted radiator gruel to eat,
and nothing else,

and just a vacuum cleaner to watch them
with its little searchlight
and voice of angry dust that remembers
when it could see
past the horizons and kitten mounds of carpet.

But today I let the bathtub overflow
so it would rain someplace
down below where the rain is dead
and hangs from the streetlamps.

I know the apartment downstairs,
a family of men named Mr. Cap
who repeat with their murmuring eyes
the obsolete pauses that once meant hello.

I hear them listening for the digital cries
of their one child,
a bag of still-moving tulips
making noises we can see once the furnace's
curfew lights have passed.

Bank of America Poem

"why am I hated by money?"
asks the man in front of me,
the bank quiet, unable to pick up
the light forgotten on the floor.

"my pockets are not criminals,"
the man continues, pulling
the teeth from his wallet.

his face moves more like the storms left behind on pennies
than the words that brought him here.

he looks around tiredly.

his eyes are evidence that he does not bleed.

"I've been off scorpions and meth
for a year," he says, taking
a book of prairie grasses
from his mauled survival bag.

"I tried to read a bible, but everyone
suffers there," he adds, handing me
a soda bottle where the sugar's run dry.

there are only two people ahead of him
but we've been standing here
long as it takes the flames
inside a wood doll to reach flashover.

his yellow iron-on shirt wrinkled and peeling.
his hairline evidence of a previous brushfire.

he starts talking louder,
"I am not a bad person. I never stole."

no one turns around.
they keep looking for the next place
in their densely populated phones,
their little holes to Baghdad.

he drops his wallet but nothing shatters.

"it's okay, it's already dead," he says and shyly looks away.

WATERGATE

You missed the one afternoon
Richard Nixon called for another
of the original Kennedy shootings.
That one dies over and over and never gets it right.
There were days when you could kill
somebody without being shot by cameras
inside the head as it explodes.
Today John Fitzgerald Kennedy
owns all the water back where he's dying still.
Today in 2007 the world is owned
by a North American sleep,
a stretch of dark road that leads into
the trees and the frog losses
and the telemarketing caves,
the headlights from unmarked cars
that leave little scars and cancers beneath your coat.
And back in the town you stay awake in,
the mailman knows everything about you.
The streetlamps know everything also.
They keep their mouths open and their eyes quiet
and creep closer to where you gnaw your spouse at night.
Forty years and your stomach is almost done
strangling you, already hideous with the slouch
of stubble from your week-long depression parties.
All a child needs to take the remaining light away
is your name and your credit card number
and a mistake from a spider's assassination hearings.
You find in the smallest regions of your cell phone
the ruins of snakes driven from the sky
and tower after tower swaying in storms of video space.
You watch for the suffering of Nixon back in the places
he no longer hears the scraps of his name.
Not Watergate, but a land ruined by peace
where he can plug in his uranium laptop both when it leaks
and when it barely shines or shows its billions
of people searching for their flesh.

In the Absence of Great Men

1.

In the absence of great men,
the governor, the smallest among us,
pays everyone who's drowned
to drag away the river
and the fingerprints of the river.

He's already slept with the dirtiest shadows of the Delaware.

He's already erased, in digital entries,
the black lung trails
between Pennsylvania mining towns.

"I was raised knowing which hand
was for voting, and which hand was for fighting," he says,

one part of a black lung tulip
his breath looking for the rape it belongs to,

the next a memory of Mohicans hunting
their eyes across the white man's tundra,
the next petal, the tundra continuing.

2.

The four surviving members of the Blairstown Democratic Club
watch the president fall farther into his tie whenever he speaks.

No language left anywhere. No one paying attention.

All worries revealed by a voice copying the other voices.

Thunder saved as cell phone data.

Words like *freedom* and *liberty* licking themselves
inside an empty Coke can floating down
the otherwise empty Paulinskill.

3.

It is cold even when little Frank Kelly draws a picture of the sun.

Panties left on the clothesline dead from hypothermia
shiver into a breeze, one of those extinction frequencies
that becomes the plowing of the afternoon sky.

4.

Children who sold their hall passes
and their souls in the nurse's office
forcing yellow jacket music
into all the edges of their bodies.

The band that sang like one lung together:
*Rain rests by falling, Rain rests by floating
home to its bucket on the moon.*

Children memorizing heart attacks and the weather that follows—
the rain wants to hurt them, but can't.

5.

In the absence of great men,
each man able to stand up
in the harsh breathing of others,

each man able to endure
his own thinking,

each man able to locate his car
at the end of the Shop Rite parking lot
and dig through the dark matter without hurting his eyes,

each man traveling far into the furnace
and the towns built inside the flames

where the fathers of the void withered overnight,

unable to survive the zero gravity
of their churches' denial seasons,
their snake-by-snake fellowship broadcasts.

6.

A woman leaves her family back in the night
few of the blizzards have abandoned.

Each snowflake a shred of the last AM radio song.

Each snowflake a disturbance in the human voice.

"During my life I was sad but not lazy," Bill Featherman said
through the static
of birds flying in long formations of decay.

MAVERICK

Inside you, the wind stops
dragging its AP wire, and the offices
wash away in the late drizzle,
newsprint smeared between heartbeats,
the halting of the family you wrote yourself.
Five years and a million silences
pass and your dying like a trilobite
goes on and on through
the impatience of stone, the weather
mostly brick where I fade and continue
inside *The FBI Nobody Knows*
and *Julia's Story* and *Maverick*.
My father, your only son, held you together
for years before your blood went still.
Neither of you spoke through the distance
of the living room, just your television
chattering with its voice of lit foliage,
and your home health aide from the Czech Republic
watching you between hurricane commercials.
You chronicled the falseness of rain in your fifty books,
and the presidents who would turn to rain, eventually
and later, Studs Terkel wrote, *Fred J. Cook, one of the ten
great muckrakers of the Twentieth Century,*
but you never told me what method to follow
in writing my own lives. Did *The Nightmare Decade*
pay for your daughter who still sneaks around in the Cold War?
I stayed close to the evening-dressed men
who looked like you: tall, black-haired, eyes
like Interlaken, collecting stories and nursing them,
combing them for the damagèd paper cotillions.

RED LAKE

I licked the raven trails from your legs
where the ground went on suffering.

The howling of guns in your eyes,
a North Dakota loneliness in your throat.

Today I wiped away my face and found
only the killings for next winter hiding there.

I shut out the sky with my black trench coat
to stop my grandfather from

speaking in shaman feathers while I
hacked away at his elbows.

And I saw the crows flailing beneath your skin,
the hitlers I was trying to breed from my own

good work. I panicked for the names I shared with you,
the native nazis now spreading under your jacket.

The other kids made fun of me because I wore
only black and was big enough to crush them

but sat there straining against my clothes instead.
I asked the boy outside the first classroom

if he believed in God and then I shot him.
I asked the girl to fondle the exact spot

on her body where coyotes had tracked
the wind, and I shot her. The security guard

with nothing but his arms held me back and held me back
before I filled him with swastikas migrating into iron.

My suicide father who now had his own place
in the broken minutes cried for me to run,

but I was still somewhere inside my last thoughts
and hearing only the black noise of deer as they fell.

Terror Song

O Lord spying from your nests
of dust and stone—
For how long have scorpions filled you—

O Lord you are a scorpion getting smaller

How many nights have only
helicopters loved us—

O Lord praying
to the landmines
for a torso to follow you,
to be in pieces the way you are
in pieces

O Lord breathing because we cannot
find your head

A mother took us into the doorway
where she lived
and showed us flowers planted
with her daughter's eye-
lashes and blackened fevers

Did she ask you for the prayer
her strongest son sweated into the desert
when the fire was a voice falling
and he could feel your blistered hair
that was still the color of water?

We washed the clouds
from your flesh
and made up words
for your charcoal kingdom

We let the suicides continue

We stole the songs from a gnat
to speak to you, Lord,
sleeping with shrapnel
in the slashed-open bowels of a lamb

We healed the land in your image, Lord,

and burned the river every time
it sinned, every time
it darkened, Lord,
like blood,

like a bomb trawling for blood
where you swam, Lord, and did not
come back for us,

the charred, still faithful
limbs we left, Lord, in the markets of avocadoes
among the fresh, coveted screams—

what you once called your children, Lord—

but you didn't tell them
the dirt and its lies
are stacked all the way to Heaven

where you cannot locate your body
scattered through the meadows
of a single commandment
of sniper fire—

Was it you, Lord, who said
to build a kingdom by closing our eyes?

Was it you, Lord, who said
that a child's fear causes nightfall?

Beware of us, Lord—

When the sunset loses another scorpion,
we feel every shard of you
shivering in your lost uranium shrines—

Terror Song (II)

A suicide boy shrieking through the plaza
            into swarms of blood
An AK-47 fired out of a mosque, its beating heart

Today the helicopters will be peeled
            right off the cloud they're eating from

A man whose head was filled
            with explosives at birth
keeps pressing his torso
            for the detonation switch
            to make the ticking stop

Dusk a dialect of incoming desert flies
Dusk the color of someone's bowels
A marine catches a boy praying
            to his rifle, singing for his father who waits
                        in the shrapnel temples of Paradise

Weak where the sun goes on touching me
            I slit my wrist and all that drips forth
                        is a bubble of saliva

A mother shakes her baby for ammo
Skinned to their souls the houses try to protect themselves
                                    with depleted uranium

The checkpoints move as the grasses move
            finished eating their fathers the sheep

The children surround me
            one of them in English

                        to make from my body a shelter
                        where God feeds all of his ashes

and his song without a head
his hands grasping together for light

caught in a sniper's crosshairs

    his kingdom
    his kingdom
    his kingdom

In Afghanistan

In Afghanistan the Hulk soaked his infected toe in a bucket
        of his green blood.
In Afghanistan the Hulk breathed for a small girl while she fell
        asleep feeling her mother for a face.
In Afghanistan the Hulk was taken by a heroin cold, a dormouse,
        a five-toed jerboa.
In Afghanistan the moon sniffed every mountain for what could
        have been the Hulk.

The gunfire between scraps of red deer frightens the Hulk.
The gunfire that wants to touch his hair suspects the Hulk inside
        each opium hideout whispered there.

On the moon that lied to him about its ability to withstand shadows
the Hulk looked for where he last lost his flesh
and on the moon haunted with cold rooms the Hulk leaked into a corner
interrupted by lightning where the lightning's father held him
while he chewed the flowers from his chest.

The day arrives with its eyes of spiders, but only if the Hulk
        falls asleep.
When the Hulk closes the great doors in his face
the butterfly with its kimono wings can search
        the tired stubble for wind.

Afghanistan remembers its trees as a cry that the Hulk would stay
behind them on a morning deceived by the dust
        and its strangers.
The child with the deepest holes in her spinal cord
        will have to be fed to the Hulk
every morning for the land to reveal where the uranium
        has turned back into sugar beets.

And the moon that was once the Hulk grows wounded inside
        its closets of slow artillery and inside the puddles that were
        like windows left broken and bloodshot through the permanent driftless war.

In the Lights of the Church-Town Earth

My mother said that God is a bad man
locked inside a cloud

Prayers come to him in birds
he tears open looking
for the blood that causes
their singing

God is not happy when we sing

I followed him for seven months
and he told me: *Get rid of your clothes
or you'll drown. Cut off all your hair
or you'll freeze. Empty the music
from your head or I won't find you*

I followed him for seven months
and his people swayed and sang
and cried in voices that were
the burning down of his kingdom

When my friend spoke in tongues
it meant a tarantula had died
and entered heaven

That is what God told me

*You will be covered in tarantulas,
they are my angels.
They will shine from you
and make truth from you
who are my smoldering*

I stayed awake during the prayer fast

I lit a match so God could see
that my body was empty
the way all of heaven was empty

I listened for my one prayer struggling in his hand

Every day the sky frightened me because
it moved and did not go away

The Sniper's Apartment

In the place I live everything I know crawls into my ears while I sleep. Tonight I listened to the man running water and turning into a shower in the apartment above ours and that is more than I have ever known about anyone in this building. You stay awake counting the number of times the snipers appear across the street in the lit windows, the lights themselves animals that never move. I sleep one day from you, where the cockroaches have weakened further from the viruses left by the exterminator. I try to give you enough of my continuous night to rest without the thirty-year-old gunshot still spreading through your arm, the Morse Code buzzer ringing next door, the late-night teenager desperate to get inside. The two cats we've had since they were little corpses jump on top of the window sill trying to see through the rips in the sky. Tonight the video surveillance camera shows the Russian man from downstairs knocking on our door. He is here to complain about the noise we make sitting at the table rubbing each other's feet, and the insect words we chant smuggling our ticking infant to sleep in the papoose we made out of old newspaper and the snow drifting from the gash in its head.

Nights of the Township Committee

To talk about the town's marijuana grid
    and compare the lengths of their

names, the committee men
    gather at the weekly meetings.

Finished, the campaigns
    of a right-wing summer.

Democrats back in their pockets
    learning to scrawl their silences again.

But this year nobody believes the speeches
    leaked by Governor McGreevey when winter fails.

A month since the Town Hall burned into a flock
    of brick clouds over Stillwater Road.

A month since the police chief
    left the scene of a high school

collision because his bowels were falling
    deep into his pants, and he smelled drunk

from where he lied about himself
    at the bottom of his beer at the Blairstown Inn.

The audience for this week's meeting,
    led by Howard Mott and the entourage

of sleep behind his pear-shaped suit,
    demand that the committee men

earn their microphone privileges
    and dismantle the police force,

who guard the town by tapping
        only dead telephone lines

and liquoring the insides of animals
        hit at 50 mph by Billy Weinbrecht, stoned

on John Deere since 1987. The men at the other end
        of a table long as the January country

nurse the rages of poisoned cattle and nod their
        eyes, their hands far away, crossing out

the agenda, fondling half-sickened Styrofoam cups,
        watching their faces melting and reforming

on the surface of the lukewarm swill.
        They agree about the "honest, regulated caffeine"

and their meetings that never ruined anyone.
        But they don't notice Tony Hipple in the front row

whose gun has fallen asleep in his mouth,
        distant as any Rumsfeld junkie

who thinks he's exposed—with one repeating epithet—
        every bomb farmer fidgeting in the aching chairs around him.

OVAL OFFICE DIARY

Homeroom Security
where one minute always gets stuck
on Monday, September 10—

The president, who now cleans the holes
from every flag there, unhispanically, says:

Only two people were tall today.

*

Leaving Crawford, Yale, the Texas Rangers,
it was hard to put food on my family,
no stamps for booze or the vintage haircuts.

*

Some may ask of me:
How many hands has our president touched
because he wanted to rest there?

*

To survive book fatigue and shot glass attacks
I've slept in the guts
of all the stuffed elephants,

(and it was more than one elephant,
I could count at least
that late).

I was always bigger than the animals.

Our men digging up deserts for the word where I went missing.

*

I think war is a dangerous place.

More room for the oceans after we frighten Islam off the map.
I'm the Decider, as you already know, and they're telling me this.

I think war is a dangerous place,

sky filled with sores and rags of misspelled cattle, spreading.

*

Important questions: how many hands have I shook,
have we made the pie high enough,
can the kids that still need to be aborted
co-exist peacefully, without food—

*

My father spoke during the day,
when none of the clouds could hurt me.

My father hired other kids to go play in the sand storm.

I hid under a scorpion.

I stayed up all night feeding my pet liver
and praying to 250 million years of coal.

I could hear the ground praying back to me
and using every word
of the dark and disorientated light correctly.

I learned my father hated my contribution.

I learned the people loved me
from someone I did not know,
who kept repeating a noise that sounded
like my name out in the honest bomb-crawling weather.

Unrecorded Population Drift

1.

North of the late promises of Christ
who died in someone else's prayers,
I haul away a stop sign's blood,

a sack of robins that fled this far,

a child watching us
beyond Newark, New Jersey,
past the shrinking headlights where winter begins.

2.

A hotel known for its half-eaten beds
crawls to the river,

a child held together with washcloths
and needles found in a mirror,

evidence of wolves (now called lymphoma).

The water tries to move on its hands and knees away from the night's rainy glare.

3.

I chew some of the violets scattered near the overpass
and they taste like my own voice.

4.

Farmers from the last light working the shade of the cell towers,
you took a pill so the moon wouldn't hurt.

You took a pill so your makers could find you again.

5.

The corporate daylight a planet with no cloud or shadow,
no grainy news shelters—

Bodies taken from a hospital's brick
creep closer to the blindness of socks missing in their empires.

6.

Undocumented population drift:

How many starvation sculptures per screen click.

How many deer know which moon to remember,
which undertow of shadowed salmon.

How many graying humans hear the clenched chains waiting,

How many already skinned to encourage a season of stillness.

How many families commanded by homeless governments
to manufacture more space
in the fathoms of a whispered nickel.

7.

Does a woman write letters to the oxygen leaving her?

Does she save the earthquake animals stranded at flashlight latitudes?

Does she document the mole shivering beyond the television chimneys?

Did she lose Odysseus behind the motel that drowned
in the gulfs of syphilis leading to Las Vegas?

9.

Wind moves through the trees
like the variations between each uncounted deer.

The leaves escape by withering to another universe.

The most honest criminal during that disturbance
warns that the human voice, even following
a pill's labyrinths, was never a safe place
to sleep or in any way remember the silence,
the temptation of a half-written heaven's golden searchlights.

My Friend the Death Legislator

Kill the phone cord slithering around the apartment
and the voices it leaves, the talking that becomes mold,
all the places you'd never look.

Kill the water that gropes you in the bathtub.

Kill the wall cracks because you feel them spreading
and your clothes for not being able to remember you.

Kill the sunlight that makes the windows hurt
and the windows for looking at you and telling everyone.

Kill the mirror by painting it the color of a black hole.

Kill the brothers and sisters you made
the nine years you lived inside dragonfly static.

Kill the clocks, they are writers of fake music.

Kill the letters that arrive, scratch
the envelopes until you can feel them twitching.

Kill the bats growing inside your computer
fill the hard drive with water and chop it into meat.

Kill the spiders who cross your body at night
broadcasting your sleep to the spider planet.

Kill the blonde girls who sing sex.

Kill the blonde girls by making them sing Paul Celan's prayers.

Kill the television, it scrawls in your skin
noises from God that you can't hear
but one day will be all that is left.

Kill the talk show host who pays people to gouge
each other with simple words
in front of a million butterflies.

Kill the million butterflies
and the rag journalists who celebrate

the weaknesses of the New England senator,
whose innards you've already dragged
out into long years of lilacs.

Pull the celebrity responsible for our destruction
from each newspaper, each magazine he or she appears in

and make each image tear at the other until not one finger
is standing. Be sure the hornets are there to finish off

whatever beauty remains. Then kill the hornets. Then kill the hornets.

GOSPEL OF SCRANTON

In the trenches of rural God
it was October and tongues fell from the trees,

the voices of Solomon breaking up the cold.

I opened my lungs
and the strangled florets dribbled forth,
coal hacked out of heart bone,

mineshaft swans returning

from the throats dug
with advancing

emphysema tactics beneath Scranton.

I heard the one who left us here
dying from the stories he started
in which none of the coal remembers him.

How hard will he have to pray,
how will he close his eyes.

Almost night, my own

arms afraid of me,
they light little disability fires
everywhere inside the ground

and sleep like deer in the earth's exposed kerosene glands.

Our only child reads from the first bone
of a girl splayed on heaven's wall
of bronchial whiskey

and ambiguous, locally controlled
television news stills.

Dark lung brokerages
offer our scattered house
at the interest rates of used, unrecognizable,
hard-to-breathe water.

Everything Today Just as the Fallout had Written

Who helps the rain
where you found the sky filled
with long grasses.

"Nobody walks there
anymore," someone says through the distance
of his own flesh.

He's the one who put the clouds together—
"Moonshine burials," he calls them.

Only the deer missing from September fellate the long grasses.

*

All summer the boxes of winter approaching
from the Asteroid Belt.
One of the boxes, one of the locked buildings,
knows where the sky's been destroyed.

But not you, hacking away the sultry rose tinder,
snow as a perimeter again.

*

The roots of your favorite tree keep the Earth from shattering.

Each time you blink, you leave
caskets in the air with no names inside them

to make a family of the endless walk in front of you.

*

Everything today just as the fallout had written—

Your body ruined by rain,
the way trees flaunt their cyanide
in certain temperatures of wind.

Your father's cough spreading under the house.

You hatched from the extermination of a rat flower,
he said with one arm haunted
by long lightning snakes.

Your father just as a man near the atomic harvest had written:

If I had my notes to the sky published
or my worst shadow,
If the doves were made of darkness again
I'd bury all the copies

exactly where you stand.

PART TWO

THE DAWN ANIMALS

I try to make myself tired by watching
the streetglow falling asleep in your hair.

Hours pass, our two little
porcupines patrol the bed

and disappear in the Manhattan
wilderness embroidered on our blanket.

I ask you if the darkness is real
and you mutter, half-asleep, that

it's the dog scratching the door in the next
apartment, which turns into a cloud at night.

I look for work inside your mouth
cleaning up the feathers my kisses left.

I listen to your eyes purring in their nests,
your lungs whispering to each other,

your thighs that make the sound
of lights dimming. I have not earned

my years of being close to you.
I steal every pilgrimage of sleep from your body

drifting away towards the blouses hanging
in the closet, all of the day's typing

waiting inside them, the arms faded
from the office's breath,

the surveillance of the colors you wear.
Don't go back to them. The dawn animals

that wrap you in their claws,
their flickering, fluorescent necklines.

THE LIFE OF A MAN WHO NEVER WORKED

Staring too long at the day's
white paint,

he feels his shirt for a heartbeat
huddled where the buffalo wardens
will never know a thing.

I worked and worked and only
the wages of the land taught me
to heal where my shadows had been crushed, he says.

A family of live bruises helps him
across the bed to South Dakota,

a church of gunshots, the moon beaten to death by children,

the horizon flattened by cattle,
arrowhead flights beyond
the grasslands and their lost Chicagos.

He tracks the tornado paths
of motels running north,

the skyline of assassin silos
withering into corn mirage,

Monsanto prairies.

He arrives at another room
painted the exact shade
and time zone as his driver's license.

I have just enough money to keep moving, he thinks,
grazing the pillows
to know who had phone sex here.

The universe, buried in his mouth,
dims through the conversation
scribbled on the nightstand:

Yesterday the trucks found me, J.B. 1997
Did they feed you well? Rex, 2000

The man who never worked
adds his own starlight that drifted
away, one sentence:

Thirty years and I've learned the wind
has more mistakes, more crawlspaces at night.

Where he's still part of Sioux Falls
he removes his clothes
and struggles not to vanish.

It is a month known only to cellophane animals.

Why are the cries nothing like plastic, he thinks.

From there he feels the mountains
that no longer pray,
the mountains cringing behind
a sheet of wind,

storms who've reached the moaning of certain stones.

He finds, between his mini-mart taco
and the Prozac he scalps for at least one authentic meal,
the exact parallel
his Laundromat bloodline was lost.

I made it as far as the dramas of a cottonwood, he says.

I advanced to the darkness of the corn when it shivers.

On television the comedians prowl
like wolves,

like the moles roaming his body,

the room abandoned here on the talk show set
of an ice machine's nitrogen-
rich loneliness.

Woman from the Village of Painted Weather

She comes from a long line of missing information.

She works at a shopping mall where she sells
tuberculosis and freight train slang
and her birth name hidden among scalped envelopes.

She doesn't come from the overnight fuel and coffee burials
or the Cheyenne River Indian Reservation.

She comes from a game played in the back
of a station wagon lost between voices
on the Great Plains. She comes from

nicotine wraiths following the wheat crops to Canada.

Her mother still awake in midnight Des Moines
with a monogamous blade of starvation grass.

And her brother and sister and father raised into livestock
behind the Chemical Bread billboard.

She builds her thoughts with pictures that mean Lakota
or less than Lakota in her obsolete prairie language.

But she does not suffer more than her shoes when they cough.
She does not wake far from the trails of shoe healers.

She follows the snow harvests, clouds huddled
like humans on the side of I-29, blown in from the fields,
waiting for the trucks to stop and heal them.

She comes from names whose blood's dried
on the underpass: Greg and Zachary and Deb,
Raven Drum and Rootbeer Eddie,
her buffalo grandparents.

Drunk on swill and Nutrasweet, she wakes
at the beginning of the back seat pastures
dug up twenty years ago in prose songs written by deer.

The story ends when she refuses
to die in the small way she's been painted into the unknown summer.

Her clothes and hair chopped in a late style of loneliness—
She is the shivering that can be felt
the moment the wind disappears.

Marion Motel, Iowa

At the Marion Motel
three flies kept the room
awake with me. Bitten

from the flowers pulsing
by the Mountain Dew machine,
they drilled through the air

songs of their tiny butchered hearts,
my arm and its scatter of bites
that wouldn't quit. I pressed my ear

against a phone number nailed
to the wall and heard what they
were doing with the towels

and the darkness of the next room.
I could hear the bed
sagging, the gasp a shirt makes

the moment it's removed.
All night while I turned
into paper, scratching notes

about the insomnia brought
by each fly, I knew that the cars
parked in front belonged

to them and that the flies
were the only ones here,
and I tried killing them

with noise from the television,
I tried killing them with snow
from an atlas of Minnesota,

I tried killing them because
the manager had left them behind,
and then I killed them

by hiding their wingprints
in my hand where I live
without a map or a horizon.

They made the fields impossible
to remember and I killed the flies
and the many cities of the flies

by shutting off their planet,
the bedside lamp, their bodies
dropping to the page

whose words, like fetuses swaddled
in mosquito's wool,
had already scratched each other

from the land itching
with sleep stains before the manager
opened his doors at dawn,

where everything ends
and he resumes his search for the flies
and their advancing forms of food.

Today on the boardwalk
a man chewing a shred of skin

Another man licking sweat
from the walls of the public restroom

Then a beach chair with a note attached:

Dear Coffin-head,
I've gone looking for you
out past the fish casinos—
When I find you
we'll start a family there

Feeding a handful of pennies to the seagulls,
each day the sky breaking
from their feathers

Today I walked and walked

I put my ear to the sand
and listened for battleships

The sun locked under the empty motel

The sea-colored nightclub almost falling in the crab-colored wind

After America (II)

At the party for the violet I took care of,
who grew one tiny lung
the day I left a window open,

The police gathered
waiting to hear beautiful
and distant truths in her breathing—

Books with words replaced by carpenter ants

Napkin flowers running the state house

A species of scab growing in New Mexico

How sunlight begins at the toes
and ends in the eyelashes,
leaving only half its information

Then the violet stopped
You were wrong, said the blackheads in the wall

You were wrong, said the soil at her feet

She never had a lung, said the flowerpot,
but the beginning of a purple moth

The police took away my house
because I lied. It didn't matter

It was warm outside and I found a footprint
where the two of us could stay

But soon the footprint would either disappear
or drag its mouth to the shores
of another human

My legs hurt whenever I touched
the violet, or what the violet had already
mistaken for conscience

Fewer places to hide from the hardening air

Soon the purple moth would die and turn against us

After America (III)

The soldiers arrive
in their platoons of algae.
They slither through the halls
of a mushroom and leave
behind the black widows
growing in their teeth.
Because there are soldiers
I put a bowl of poison on my steps.
I make my pillow tell me
they're not here at all.

The soldiers hack the wings off mosquitoes.
They fill the moon with the black ink
they carry in their heads.
I sleep with a shovel.
In the morning I will bury
the night birds who mauled
each other without cries.

But tonight the soldiers find me
and bring down my walls of skunk cabbage,
my moss hive, the castle I built
out of crackerjacks and bread mold.
I burrow deep into the ice box
where their eyes can't reach.
The soldiers empty the bed
with their tiny bayonets.
They fill the answering machine
with parts of the wind
they've taken hostage:

We will steal the rain from your eyes.
We will stay in your head
with its rocks and arsenic.
We will rape the coyotes

living behind your breastbone.
We will follow the canals in your hands
to where the animal factories
and the spring breezes begin.
We will take back the marigold's color,
the flight patterns of grain, all of the singing,
and we will feed the half-opened deer
with your lice, your bruises, the fear left
of your stomach, everything that can be
detected by your abandoned and butchered lamps.

AFTER AMERICA (IV)

Here the tanks creep by
dressed as children,
the war lurching

through artificial spaces
in the weather. The platoon sleeps
while a mother searches

her body for her missing son
and the father skins the rugs
for dinner. "Even though they're

quiet, those troops sound
like dogs goring each other,"
he says, and hands over his dead

credit cards and existence
licenses cut up and used
as bread. The humidity,

which begins as a blacksnake,
fills the mother's plate.
Their one daughter joins the war

because it's promised her food
and protection against
the dark noise of the heat.

Our leader stays strong ravaging
us from the television
broadcasting more walls meant

as a world, the father's bed haunched
like an animal to guard
what's left of the moonlight.

The daughter knows each
drop of water is awake,
each drop of sand.

And out back, in the sweltering
web space, butterflies
have fallen, each raped

and resuscitated by soldiers
in the dandelion's
shorn and blinding shade.

The President I Love

On television my president falls asleep
tracing the head of a nickel.

He finds the moon in the Oval Office
and doesn't know where it belongs or what to say.

My president writes a memo to his pants,
puts it in his pocket and worries when they don't respond.

My president stands tall as the millipede
where the blueprints for Alpha Centauri are kept.

My president stays in bed thinking about his five words,
the cries they make when the microphone is off.

My president sneaks around carrying an envelope
filled with heatwaves and changes in the weather.

When he speaks, my president remembers the bible verses
we shared at the bottom of the Mississippi.

Today I shake my president's hand and he greets me
with sentences he used before there were people.

My president picks the prayers from his teeth, and we listen.
My president fills his daughters with humidity, and we listen.

He studies battle plans among a focus group of oil derricks.
My president who drinks orange blossoms

from the foot of an infected Arab
and tells men squatting in camel shade

that he's making water and land and freedom.
My president who captures their father,

their maker holding himself in a foxhole of desert sun.

The Song of Iraq

I saw the sheik wiring his beard with explosives.
I saw him leading young foxholes out of a journalist's slit-open throat.
I saw his sons at Pak Punjab eating tomatoes that were improvised movie devices.
I saw him burying heartbeats in the sidewalk.
I saw him burying heartbeats he cut from a burqa.
I saw his daughters feeding a camel to abandoned marines.
I saw the sheik burning in the desert and praying that his god of cadavers
    sleep here in the oasis he built out of figs and humans
    who found their song before death.
I saw him reading to the sand he gouged out of his own skin.
I saw him take to bed each grain until each grain had a name.
I saw the sheik hiding in the mosque scorpions he made children with.
I saw him unrolling his women and gutting them for prayer.
I saw his daughters and sons swaying in the henna leaves, forgotten.
I saw the sheik beg forgiveness from a cobra for kissing the kohl
    around a woman's eyes.
I saw him at dawn circling Fallujah, the soldiers asleep in his turban.
I saw him circling Fallujah at dawn, eating blood from the helmets left behind.
I saw his mother offering her hands to the sheep, who stayed alive
    on their coats of smoldering fleece.
I saw the sheik cleaning his leg with a tooth he found in the piles
    of tank treads.
I saw him running away with goats no one is looking for.
I saw him knocked down by old women carrying vegetable sacks.
I saw his father put his ear to the ground and I saw the sheik was part of the
    ground where ears were growing on strands of jasmine.
I saw the sheik holding the Euphrates in a blanket and leading it back to
    Najaf and Karbala and Sadr City.
I saw him pulling acacias from babies sleeping together in a mass of
    pulsing dirt.
I saw him turn into a mango tree at sunset, and the black-dressed mullahs
    and rebels eating from his groin.
I saw the sheik lighting a palm leaf so his god would be able to find him.
I saw the sheik leading his locusts to a day of paradise fires.
I saw him leading souls that had become brothers by stone, young boys
    whispering to cool their lips while they marched.

I saw his sons pounding on the walls inside a clay shard.
I saw his daughters pounding on the walls of their shadows.
I saw the sheik taking off his robes and letting the tongues out of his chest.
I saw the sheik taking off his head and his neck and letting the mob
	track his footprints back to the sky he dug for them.

PART THREE

from The Damnation Psalms Of Saint Halutzie

I failed all my life at defending what I loved and now Hell exists
because I said too much back in your garden
of gowns that the tulips destroyed.

Hell darkens to the color of your sleep when the final fallen petal
refuses to reveal how to find the tulip that fears
the ticking of the tulip beside it.

But in Heaven, everyone works because they've been promised food.
There is one deer in all of Heaven, and it bleeds.

To find rain I have to dig far into the ashes.

I make lists of the names of children I am afraid of
until they can no longer endure the shadows they've protected.

In Hell, men wash the moths from each other's clothes
and spread brief zephyrs by shutting each other's eyes.

In Heaven a small boy cuts flames out of black construction paper
because the singing hurts.

I sing only of Hell, the book of granite lilies
where you impregnated the flowers who felt nothing but
the distance of the dirt when it no longer sang.

Who was it that made the earth's insides the shape of a human body?

In Heaven my breathing frightens away the starlight.

There is beauty here, but the angels are dead and trembling in their feathers.

NOTES FROM THE ATROCITIES OF THE LAND

Pray to what you've already lost of your life

Follow the antelope on days with no sky

The lean-to a month's journey if you follow the right suffering

Do not return to the holes of the closed and lurking desert malls

Go past the rain where heaven's rotted, that trap set by the janjaweed

Head out to where it's darkest but do not leave any shadows behind you

It is not against what's already written to drink from your handful of raw
bullets

Do not trust the wind where no grasses move; it is not wind but arson

And though you hear the sun decaying in your eyelashes from certain
distances

Do not stop for the dismantling of the black-haired sand

Or the tribes of dust who've been erasing you with their millions of eyes

Do not help the mosquito's daughter who wants you to use her malaria fevers
for sleep

63

Do not pick up the fallen clouds the hyenas have gnawed open trying to find
water

Drape a blanket over the body of God who threw away the blood of the one
who left Him here

Stone Snow After You Wandered

Wind mauling your body
for bread, deer made of bread
and not blood, the sun a drop
of someone else's brain
trembling on a bare branch,
the branch's shadow made of endlessness,
not bread, not blood stalking the stone snow.

*

Who is that,
speaking in crooked mouths
behind the book of bricks
and famine developments.

Who is that,
speaking in church bulletins.

Who is that, spider-quiet
since the beginning of the world,
speaking in snakes at the snake ovens.

*

Unemployed, you have to live
where an eyelash lived.

Unemployed, an eyelash's bed
blown miles from the face,
miles from the eye's cold and twitching city.

*

Take zyprexa, say the geese.
Take zyprexa, say the zebras.
Zyprexa to make you
more like your colleague
the asparagus, more like your
maker the asparagus.

*

An amateur, I paint the shreds of a horse
into an afternoon with no water.
Each shred trying to reach where it's been
shorn from the blood maps.

Each shred trying to leave Bangladesh.

Bangladesh after Bangladesh
in the searchlight
of a broken mosquito.

AFTER RUSSIA

1.

In the submarine puddles
we came to a dry place
far from sleep
where periscopes moved
like bones of rain.

Your gulags
carried an animal silence
in which none of the snow
was lost.

Teeth ringing through the cold war deer theater,

we'd made it to where the trees hated
each other at the end
of their human shadows.

"We'll never be here as people again."

2.

We stood where the ground
and its wars became
too small to remember,

and the trees and rifle fire kept falling,

wet with a leaf's
one surviving shard.

"It doesn't matter how long
we loved the people
from where we slept," you told me,

and that a back room's monsters knew
the exact place
the screams on each leaf went
and that they would
never tell.

3.

You exchanged a winter's wandering
while we detonated tunnels
in search of that very siege.

We interrogated the eyes of every house.

The vodka corrected the sky's color
deep in its arsenal
where no sky was found

and the days ahead were giggling
between the hooves of children

who no longer drank
now that the bullets with
mongrel bears inside them
had been worshipped and boiled
together in their caves.

SAND SONG OF MESOPOTAMIA

Today I wrote a song in which Israel moved its militia into a pregnant woman's bed.

Today I wrote a song in which a shoe, and all the sinews enslaved to that shoe, were filled with swarms of infant IEDs.

Today I pollinated a song whose final flower with petals of butterfly warheads fled Iran.

Today I praised a song for the babies born with six mouths, six legs, six skinless stomachs, and a six-billion year half-life inside the furnace of every Iraqi sand tear.

Today, by destroying a song, I made sure there were enough beds and chairs to blunt a room's nothingness, which means a never-ending scorpion's thirst, its memory of the desert that doesn't die.

Today I stole a song in which the homeless built houses and raised families and food that will continue growing inside their sunburned entrails.

Today I blamed a song in which the Midwestern snow originated from a drone's healing circle many Pakistans away.

Today I excavated, from a plant's groin, a song that infected the Madonna Mafia with a melodic sequence of sonar terrorism.

Today I exchanged a song for the terrorist elephants, the terrorist giraffes, the terrorist oxygen, the terrorist fern forests, the terrorist mercies of medicinal marijuana, the terrorist sunsets, the terrorist shark sleep, the terrorist carrots and celery and kale that do not leave the body, the intestinal photos of the Gaza Strip taken from the cries of a leaking child, the war on shadows, the war on people who find enough to eat without having to plant pancreatic spores in the hells of the soil, the creek bed Lakota whose fully-subsidized hack drinking earns the status of enemy activity, and though I saved his name on a dollar that trusted me once, I won't discuss the terrorist child helping a turtle find its little door in the terrorist grass.

Today I climbed to the top of a song that hid the houses inhabited by live chess pieces pillaged for money that can't be comforted or fed or held in the hand.

Today I developed a song for the water as it died.

Today I protected a song for the water as it was ridiculed.

Today I harvested a song for the water hidden one carbon minute away in the mirages that revealed another child thriving from dehydration.

In the song I can locate the Syrian helicopter nests.

I can count all of the wind's bodies.

I can count and remove those who've made it to the gas chambers of heaven.

In the song I can count the salvations taken from a child's amputated leg and copy the Western patriotism that nourishes from far away his dirt dinners and his bomb wiring and the syringes used for drinking and for putting the rain back together.

I can abandon that song by deleting the shadows the child leaves unchecked as he crawls through the artillery-cold heroin forests of Afghanistan.

I can dismantle the song by betraying each bird when it sees the child leading his headless animals into the cruel churches of my hand.

Today I beat the last song to death with a bullet casing I stole from the rubble of all the songs that would never make anyone happy again.

Today I felt no remorse for the songs and their misplaced blessings.

Today I reported both hands for their terrorist ambitions—the one that grows its own grain and the one condemned for hiding every song inside the dust hospital where God sleeps by himself with the only feather that survived.

Today I promised I would protect his otherwise secure kingdom, safe because it remains empty except for the sins of a wood thrush weeping.

Roundup Insurgency

Harold ties his own bomb-sniffing nooses.
"We don't call them shoes anymore," he says.
The dust records everything they do here.

"We have a national holiday
for the afternoon the dust turned
into everyone's traitor, and that day is every day."

"The nights are against the law
because that is when our thoughts
come for us," Harold says.

"And though we try, we cannot turn off
the television where the gutted
money's gotten taller."

His father repeats one word:
Monsanto. Monsanto. Monsanto.
"It keeps memory—all memory—from

finding him," Harold's sister Nina says.
The handgun party came yesterday for the mother.
They arrested her for choosing

to let her uterus devour the rest of her body.
Harold flaunts how the ravenous,
thought-dark shoes amputate,

toe by toe, the planet under his feet.
"Our father lost the last safe place in his head
and we're next," Nina says.

Outside, flocks of searchlights
take over the sky. "Each person gets assigned
a baby searchlight," Harold says,

preparing a meal of splinters and salted nails.
"We can lose weight now," he says.
"We can look like beautiful, worshipped cadavers now."

Sports Illustrated propaganda.
"Pornography For The People!"
(a mother nursing her infant's vaccinated

button that cures faraway tracking errors)
(a father impregnating his daughter the moment she's born)
(filling her with baby searchlights).

And when a man begins to cry,
his throat grows venomous thorns
and needles and spines that can be cured

only in the flesh-eating hospitals
(and visits there, like subsidizing a celebrity's
snake sugar vineyards

among the chances of heaven,
are also mandatory).
The stomach has its own cameras.

"Soon we will have to eat what crawls
out of us," Harold says while his mouth drags the rest
of his shadow to a different room.

And when he says his hands will eat every saddened thing
on her body, Nina tames her sudden smile,
already transmitted to the programmers

of live starvation quizzes. Some days Harold grows food
at the bottom of his forced happiness
and some days the food tastes like that happiness.

Today, Harold holds Nina's hand.
Today, they listen for their mother's improbable return.
Today, their father sits in a corner chewing a spider.

Monsanto.
Monsanto.
Monsanto.

In the Months Before the Police State

Forgotten by the lamplight
and the snowman I slept with

I've burned the rumors out of my clothes.

The cloud marshals who no longer reach my window
led away in deer hides.

Thoughts that know nothing about me
migrate to the ends
of my blood.

The trees take pictures of my soul.
The trees now racks of eyes.

I follow the snow scars
made by slaughtered angels
until I find a mouth where I can rest.

And filled with the thirty-five years
of vacuum cleaner noise

and flocks of mist over the video plantations

I make myself die a little
by disturbing the reflection
on the surface of my coffee.

Someone else pretends
by eating a sandwich that he won't
report anyone.

I chop down cigarettes
in the dead of the walmart slums
and only part of me gets arrested.

The wind gropes the oldest among us first—

I don't know what else to say
now that words fall over in the street
instead of people.

Just that the sky crawls north,
into what was once the ground.

Inauguration Assignment

Write a poem a brick will enjoy as it softens and leaks into your
head, where, out of self-betrayal, you trust every meaning of
the word *change*. Write a poem that will nourish the flag-wet
page as it gives up its territory. Write one poem cursing for
peace and one poem listening for innovative ways to destroy
what hurts nothing. Write a poem in which you voted for an
unmarked colossus and one in which you voted for a person
already duplicated in Microsoft sunsets. Write a poem where
food and all memories of food driven from the soil can survive.
Create punctuated denials of the food's warlords, each chemical
deleted with strategic misspellings. Also include people and
enough hatred between flowers to be convincing. Beware of
what you leave out. Lighten but do not edit the stains of a
day's praise trapped in each person's eyes. Think ahead by
three gunshots. Plan for the words already behind you. They
know things. Remember the holes in every name whose liberty
cannot be exhumed. Bring enough measurable distances of a
rainforest's dense daylight into what you decide to write and
what you decide to omit out of kindness for those who do not
listen. Write in only one true direction. List every citizen killed
in Iraq, every child in Afghanistan. Also each rictus cry of white
phosphorus and each stone that's been occupied and each day of
nothing but dust. Try your best to transcribe the predator music
played from Beethoven drones in Pakistan after Pakistan after
Pakistan. Make a place for laughter and anger and those who
despise what you do. Point to where commas can be seen in the
sky that always ends differently. Write with live insects instead
of letters. Eulogize the homicides and forgotten velocities of
Christmas as it approaches. Make the rich forgive those who
are not rich. Make the poor forgive those who are not poor. Do
not write on the page so much as stain the page in a way that
cannot be taken back. List all the ways the sun can be divided
into strips of land. Name all the computer diseases and how
each is a separate country whose people survive only by hating

with clichés chosen for their forced compassion and Hallmark brutality. And knowing this, write a love poem. Make sure to use an ink whose dampness can be controlled. Draw a map whose rivers can be traced to each child conceived. Know that if they've been recorded as data, the kisses from which the children started will be traded for one more night and will never be thought of again. And from a place that cannot be remembered, write a love poem to each nonexistent thing. Remind the people that winter is now as warm as the interrogations of a freeholder when he visits those who've cast their enemy votes. Remind them there is no proven method to forgive a gun for its mistakes. Remind them to sleep while sleep is still possible. Write a poem whose words are truly in love, like the ones who left them here back in the days of words. As for the people, write a list of those who deserve to live.

When the day arrived on which I'd be destroyed, I put on all the clothes I could fit onto my slight frame. Early summer and already shriveling from the heat brought on by the gypsy moths, I wanted the protection of being large as possible for the end of my life, which would be today, now that I had finished my afternoon meal and the three men emerged from the basement where for the past week they'd been going over their final details. The man in charge was obese and had knots in his face and read only the newspaper that our small town published, and therefore knew everything about me from the letters I'd written. The other two men, one tall and the other of medium height, both of them with shadows falling where their eyes should've been, kept silent behind the man in charge, who said my demise would be a matter of them moving together when asked and saying nothing. I offered the man in charge a glass of water that I made myself the day before and he drank it, saying that I possessed good manners for someone who was already gone. "What do you mean?" I asked. "Your assassination, it's been taking place since we arrived," he said. I noticed that my arms and legs still listened to me; I could see myself, the three men, the room, all of us together in the same mirror; and my layers of clothing felt like the touch of a beautiful and voluptuous woman. "Why do you look so happy?" the man in charge asked. "I didn't know I could be this comfortable in summer," I answered. "How can you feel with so many clothes?" the man asked. "Each of my six shirts knows a different and wonderful pleasure," I said, "like waterfalls who understand the rain on Maui." A knot fell out of the man's face and the shorter of the two silent men immediately picked it up and put it back in its place. "Why do you insist on your well-being after a week of slow annihilation?" the man in charge asked, motioning for his helpers to remove my clothes. "My body has never felt this close to me, and I have never been so close to those who've killed me before." The two silent men removed my shoes, my three pairs of blue socks, the first layer of sweatpants filled with miles of running, then my blue jeans and cobweb underpants, there was nothing I could do, only my shirts were left, who had memories they'd never shared with me. "How do you feel now that your shirts are leaving you?" the man in charge demanded. "Like the small man who survived writing letters filled with champagne trees that died of happiness." "What will be left of you, now that you're dead?" he demanded, louder. "A new person filled with the world I loved because you were kind to me, licking away my organs only while I slept, talking to me so I could experience the last of my words."

Summer Broken Behind the Searchlights

You write the word "happiness" and wait for the alcohol decay of autumn,
when the outdoors once again repeat the moods of motels wandering from Seattle,
not as a place, but a memory of self-asylums and shoplifting.

You hold in your hand a flower that's been broken since August.

      Ten leaves in your crumpled pocket.

      Seagulls impaled all over the sky.

      Worthless
      wind currencies.

    Your woman wraps her body with a child's plastic entrails for protection.

    "I can no longer feel my blood," she says.

The homelier buildings undress and send their eyes to the river, men who look like yo
washing with hard water the $2 books they made.

    You hear wind moving the nightclubs of New Jersey closer.

    Not music, but the sound pigeons make shutting their storefronts.

Pot-bellied with a beer child, your lightheaded jacket collapses against the pavement
beneath you.

    "I had one book, and I couldn't stop touching it," you confess to your woman.

    No one holds the illegal and mostly memorized dance dealers accountable,
    nor the trattoria ensembles who share the secret locations of 1996:

    A second, third, and fourth search that was told, each untalented karaoke
night,
    "You sure have guts, singing out loud like that."

You survived the faux-superiority of a noise-writing Rutgers prodigy who said,
"Individuality is the most insidious conformity." He lasted for as long as it takes blood
to dry.

Not the required five years of commercial self-hatred.

You fall to the sidewalk where three, maybe four people live,
Orion missing its one lit stairwell.

THE SONG OF THE WATER PLANET

The water is a lie.
The water will be blamed for its own disappearance.
The water flows to us from the basements of the earth.
The water goes brown in its invisible cities.
The water moves with expeditions of punctured tarpaulin.
The water breeds only uncountable and useless water.
The water will be punished for revealing its unforgivable information.
The water will be poisoned and devoured by human lobsters.
The water will return because there are no other gods.
The water will be given only the protection of the pelican word for "water"
        while it weakens with the stillness of all plankton.
The water's father will be fed the lost laughter of a hermit crab.
Treat the water as an animal flowing with cellophane mist.
Invest in the toxic potentials of water.
Buy and sell water!
Predict the prices of water, the demands of the crowds of water.
If water does not advance, then water will be killed.
None of the water is new.
Water is an old and hackneyed master.
Water is less valuable than television movies of ice.
Water is less valuable than a dress pregnant with octopus.
Water is less valuable than men fighting in cell phone pictures.
Water that can be thought of as a vertebrate now.
Water that can be heard when its bones of a thousand windows point
        toward the sky.
There are no longer spaces between people and the red robot sounds
        of water.
There are no longer sanctuaries of benevolent water in the petroleum eternity.
There are no longer songs whose water has never been touched.
There are search towers instead of oxygen on the microscope slides
        of slowed river water.
The water cannot be trusted: it is no longer a proven place of healing.
The water cannot be trusted even when our spies have infiltrated
        the fish cameras of algae hotels.
The water can't be tasted: it can be guessed at, but never known.

The water's people will have no water to drink, no water to cut open
        for the deeper water.
They will have to sip the false glacier melt from their own parched bodies.
They will forget the lakes and reservoirs and underground oceans of fog.
The water can be discussed, but only in leviathan apocrypha.
The water can be felt as pain because the insides of the water
        are turning human now.
The water is despised, the water is overcrowded, the water is herded
        and forced into plastic bottles with no mother, no father,
        not a word or a prayer or a breath from the next labeled
        crack of light.
The water can be listened to because its molecules are thickening
        from a horrible thirst.
The water is not dying, the iron people will tell you
        while the water cowers in the bottomless aquifers of antifreeze,
        unable to move the heavier water, unable to reach the iron surface
        where the ships are not afraid and the sonar is an advancing predator
        that survives now in fleets of shark memory.
No one listens to their weeping that can be drilled and tested and taken away.
No one feels the stronger water nuzzling
        the weaker water during the body's mutilation dramas.
How will anyone survive the stillness of water,
        how will anybody endure the secrets among the water's many selves.
Each person betrays, through a blunted thirst, his or her graveyards of rain.
Each person hears and ignores—as difficult, wasteful, and unproven—
        the cries of the dark and falling water.

PATRIOTISM

10 A.M. and already 90 degrees,
a woman spreads the insides

of a burst trash bag across
the sidewalk and sits

down in it, muttering about having
to find a kiss, or a hole

where people leave their kisses.
It's in this pile somewhere,

she says, but not with her mouth.
Maybe she keeps away

whatever will find us, I thought,
still sore from the noise

dragged down my street
the night before

by the bar scouts
and the muggers out late.

When the temperature hits
anger, there is no

woman, only the sacks of smashed
eggs and oatmeal blockages

moving the way
clothes used to move.

The brain cancer
generation lured vaguely

toward the corner grocery emptied
to nothing but a repeating

car alarm,
a fire engine's cry,

the yelling of a cab driver
who's side-swiped another

cardboard box where
someone sits at her window

cursing the heat, pulling scrap metal
from her vagina,

emptying her body and eating it.

HEADLINE SONG: MARCH 19, 2003

Manhattan stormwalk,
silver couple

holding hands
deeply

discover new coffee,
neighborhoods

made of thunder
and mice turning

wheels where one can
drink from the trees,

and early fireflies
crowd the sky on every

television feeling
for feathers

and arrivals in the late
rain—

the homeless man names
his daughter after

a damaged rose drifting
back to its nest—

the kindergarten next door
sings in wet sentences

quiet, quiet
as the Iraqi shoe family

hiding

in a pothole this
third stormday,

spring still the nonsense
in a car alarm's mouth

two blocks away.

BORDER PERSON

I wake up cold
where my clothes

had been, their pockets
and imagined faces

a gang of lanterns
tracking wolves.

No more dawn
in my slaughtered country,

I run the bathroom water,
scrape the sleep from my lips;

River to the next town
freezing in the mirror,

Snow drifts across
the 25-watt ceiling,

I dismantle the desk lamp,
the television,

the ten-dollar deer shivering
in my blanket,

one more father bleeding
whiskey from his antlers

tracks me to this motel,
his last fawn letting

me explore with my night lily
inside her while she turns

to static in my bed
of thinning moss.

PART FOUR

The Undermining of the Democratic Club

Deer gather under the bridge
exchanging hoofprints.
A man at the Agway platform
teaches his son how to stack
the burlap corpses of chicken feed.

There's no money in the Blairstown newspaper
or the failed McDonald's
led away in the middle of the night.

The election signs for F.D. Shotwell,
Township Committee, have crawled into the road
and taken the place of black ice.
None of his traffic lights are awake.
None of his democrats see him alive in bed,
covering his heart attack with blankets
and flickers of raw *New Jersey News 12*.

The high school covens drink from each other
in the A&P parking lot
and chant for the midnight stock clerks
to come help them drown.

The police scrape through the river
tracking their chief who blackmailed Art Huff
with all the doors left open inside his child-angry wife.
They hear gang colors of wind approaching from Newton.
Close to the crimes of the water table,
the town's one detective swims quickly under the shotgun trees.
The sound of his eyes clenching reaches the Christian cell towers.

He knows one thing: the river steals
its current from what's been spoken here:
We've run out of money for sunlight.
The mayor's body is empty.

The river sneaks past the dying houses
and the amphibian town halls.
It whispers to food-frightened Emma Cramer: *Eat. Please. Eat or die.*

And one trout minute away, a boy follows those rumors
until he's just an interruption in the current,
the searchlights thinning to arsenic where he floats.

THE LIVES OF WALLFLOWER MOUNTAIN ASH

Last night I broke into the town hall,
police sirens looking for somebody
one election away on the floor of a pothole.
Last night I drank daffodils and radio fizz
and reversed the Republican voting records.

The Township Committee confiscated
my voice, replaced it with black flowers
caught in the gears of a backhoe,
wallflower mountain ash kept as carnations
for the high school rape ceremonies.

Freeholder Walter Orcutt said the sky
was spraypainted by democrats
over the First United Methodist Church
to confuse the East Avenue leukemia families
butchering the traffic signals for warmth.

Darkness cut up by kids barking,
my parents out in the woods running
for office, I walked through the shadows
dead since kindergarten and followed the sleep
spread by the mayor who cut himself

each night, the mayor who shouted
for the destruction of the PTA mother
who ran away with the land, the hard-singing
crocuses a day before the coming democracy,
the clean and suspicious water,

the frogs that meant no harm,
a dumpster bruised open behind Dale's Market
where we ate from our rejected children
and stayed without light,
the town silent, the televisions turned off.

We voted against any compassion that could be
traced back to us. We tried to drive away
our names, our birth numbers and billing addresses,
animals without hope in the tar sands
of someone's charred and flickering screen.

After America (V)

Outside the strip mall lunch trap,
the policemen eat from buckets
of their own pancreatic juices.

We grow guns now instead of food.

The money I keep shivers
because there is not enough.

On the radio no one is allowed to breathe
and speak at the same time,
but somehow that war ends
and maybe one voice linked to solar flares
makes the sky's dead water
seem safe enough to determine the direction
of the Kardashian aqueducts.

The caterpillar I stole from its leaf
crosses my motel room
and follows the lights of jackrabbits
abandoning North Dakota.

The money I keep trembles
because I use the same eyes its father used.

The inebriated combines
cry from their tavern outside Fargo:

Fracked waitresses and little green bottles of extinction.

A neighbor burns down his children
to keep his house from leaving,
and hobbles through a night of television:

Wind out of the broken buffalo grasses,
a man caught lurking inside a woman,
the news anchor coughing himself
to whatever word's been prohibited.

I travel for days into the hills on my computer screen
looking for someone to marry,

and meet only strippers
eating sticks and holding back their breasts,
the miles of silicone encouraging
nothing but money.

I talk to them with my flesh far away in my hands,
the only kind of communication allowed.

By then each organ has dried into dollar bills.

By then summer turns obsolete
as their bodies waste away, alone,
to their diaper-shriek harems
and classic rock penitentiaries
and crank bug palaces
where every sore is special and easy
to fuck and fill with children.

After America (VI)

A man sells used pornography
outdoors a block from K-Mart,
wind where his face used to be.

A woman on the street molesting her shadow,
howling SAVE OUR SUNSET
when she comes to her building scrawled
in the East River.

The stripper, missing for a whole Christmas,
cowers inside pigeon feathers
where the dead sunlight shines.

The curry breathing of taxis continues
beneath the skin hours after
a person awakens into the workday sleep.

A tabloid author pays
to have the year's gossip scraped
from the crotch of his writing hand—

It is a good minute for winter—
The Flatiron Building with room
for only one more book,
and none of that minute's hate speech.

A word spoken by one man
becomes a word spoken by another,
and continues east of Grand Central
word by word until some undefined thing
arrives at the end of the bus line

whose fleets of kabob vendors
can be seen rowing into the greasy Atlantic.

The trains to Far Rockaway dissolve in their tunnels
and emerge as different trains,
each passenger slower by one mantra.

And as a last resort,
workers locked in their laptop offices
exchange blessings hacked from a seagull
protected by live windows
lost and regrouping between blisters of rain.

No Words at the Press Conference

Bald eagles fall asleep under the president's tongue,
his legislations fluttering past his feet
and onto the ground programmed with handclap chasms.

Everywhere he walks the air brightens with pain,
which reveals a hesitation between facts
and the trick lighting of the teleprompter.

He hides in a hole in the tax code
when the alien storm corporations report
losses of lightning over the hell countries,

no electricity for the angels growing there,
no lamps to keep the gray tulips awake,
not one vein stitching the prayer robes together.

The president writes that he doesn't know
how to make the bald eagles remember America.
Eleven words that keep returning to his March cabinet.

And on TV the president seems the shade
of a bird's cry, the bird itself gone, now just
a random twitching in the president's head,

its inebriated libraries gutted and made into penthouses,
every species of dirt and Christian darkness
thriving where the sky used to go on for weeks.

The Song of America

I'm raising my child to become the end of rotting,
      and to expose the lushness of the cemetery moth.
I'm raising my child to know the difference between the two sunsets:
      one purple with thermonuclear iodine,
      the other the charred insides of rain.
I'm raising my child to find the stones his brothers fed each other.
I'm raising my child to fall behind the apricot blossoms
      and to trust only others who've fallen behind.
I'm raising my child to listen: there is so much noise
      only silence will be remembered.
I'm raising my child to fill in the spaces between wars
      and the spaces between people
      where everything grows even after the last space is gone.
I'm raising my child to bring into the world books that suffer
      with words detention-kids make over and over.
I'm raising my child to follow the scatter of flesh across the sky,
      birds and their wingprint trails to Alaska.
I'm raising my child to predict the sicknesses left of summer
      by the number of shadows he sweats.
I'm raising my child to plant pennies where he'll find rest
      and good fingerpaint for one night.
I'm raising my child to chop down the televisions of peasants
      and their machine that picks thunderstorms from a leaf.
I'm raising my child to write a treaty for his own smells,
      the ones that hurt the self and the ones that hurt others,
      and a treaty for the poison sumac whose only emotion is hunger.
I'm raising my child to dress like a long line of near-humans
      if he wants to be recognized
      and to show kindness to the roadkill that sneaks into his bed.
I'm raising my child to know which part of a hamburger is still afraid.
I'm raising my child to be captain of the abandoned mail trucks
      and to lead the grasses across the Midwestern sleep.
I'm raising my child to leave New York.
I'm raising my child to add letters and numbers to his name
      and chameleons and hellbenders behind his name.
I'm raising my child to drown and to drop dead and to carry buildings
      on his back.

I'm raising my child to listen to his face breaking when it's cold.
I'm raising my child to seduce only photographs of women.
I'm raising my child to know that the cobras that shiver
          in the sky at night are mistakes and not responsible for us.
I'm raising my child to leave bread for the voices that come after dark.
I'm raising my child to keep his eyes closed.
I'm raising my child to tell the truth by having no sound at all.

Human Flowers

I follow the Korean girl talking to sparrows on her cellphone.
I follow her because there are flags nuzzling the tenement roof
    and I cannot sleep.
She has hair so black that I forget the fire engines
Pulling their sirens through sleeping pillows.
I want to ask her if she knows she is going to die.
I don't know how long I follow or how far.
She moves like a curtain, an exotic dandelion
    bringing fevers in her neck.
The buildings keep changing into the color of her skin.
Her shoulders are almost gone, they are that small,
    they must hold all that's left of winter.
The sounds she creates are beautiful because I understand nothing.
I follow the sparrows washing up on the beach of her tongue.
I follow her through the puddle-eyed ruins of the Bowery,
Past the man chopping his fingers, the man who sleeps standing up,
Whose head must be filled with condors grazing in vaults.
I follow her to the Jones Diner
Where a forklift operator scrapes the eyes from a traffic signal
    and mumbles that he's a terrorist.
She walks to Pakistan, a deli at the end of the block.
There are secret chambers everywhere the sidewalk touches her feet.
I follow her because her grocery sacks are ticking.
I follow the boots that hold her together.
I follow because she hides me from the sky
That falls every day closer to the Hudson.

Countries Between My Closet and the Subway

And I decided today that I would not hurt,
I walked to the subway and watched the color
Of each person's eyes and this is something
I have never done and I walked on a sidewalk I have
Never walked and it was a new and wonderful country—
Trees crayoned by children to match the shape
Of their favorite parent, languages whose letters
I do not know, people with their own music,
And I saw a pony, or a man who resembled a pony,
In the back seat of a taxi running a red light, and
I decided today that I would not hurt because
The orchestra of car horns is the noise of the world hurting,
And I took a batch of ten percent discount flyers
For ladies' shoes from the Hispanic woman
At 43rd and 5th and dumped them in the trash
Three blocks away where she couldn't see
And her bosses would never find them;
Everything meant I was going to live—
The buildings sprouted into blossoms because it was
Spring and the accountants and receptionists
Dragged trains of pollen into their office-space,
And a boy stood on top of the Lincoln Building
Making rain with his mouth and there was meaning
In the tabloids, even if the rain didn't last
Enough for me to finish reading the stories
And I died somewhere in the pictures, I've dressed
In my strongest blue eyes for the woman I love,
I've given the same man eighty cents each morning
For a persian danish, and I decided today
I would not hurt, and I moved to the song
Of a crowded mother answering her street phone
And soothing the Harlem River with words
And children between words that were never here at all.

Today, while out walking with Stephanie, it occurred to me that I didn't hate people, but was deathly afraid of them. The success of others scared me; no matter how modest, I marveled and shook at the apparent victory of the vendors and the delivery boys and the deli clerks. The prostitutes and the panhandlers had a dignity like acorns fallen from a tree and still intact long after the tree had been burned and dragged away. Collectively, they were like ants or spiders, but with the stink of self-importance without which the city would crumble into its network of manholes. It all seemed very frightening since I didn't have a part in the workings of the city other than my contribution of breath and observation. I worried what they would do to me once they got word of my inertia.

The fruit-seller on 45th Street was yelling something I couldn't understand; his voice sounded like a dissonant violin echoing underground from one of the city's ossuaries where construction workers and subway conductors were filed away without flowers or prayers. Above the street there were many open windows like vacant eye sockets behind which women were ironing sweaty shirts or sleeping or making love without air conditioning in the hundred degree humidity. I could hear a nylon-string guitar, Villa-Lobos or something flamenco playing behind a curtain somewhere above my head, close to the sky. The festive quality of the swift delicate music frightened me. I have never known how to have fun. We passed bars and restaurants; their patios were open, and people sat at tables consuming expensive and mediocre delicacies, and their laughter was like snakes crying inside their teeth because they were laughing about the end of the world.

I was a vagrant in waiting. We kept walking and I thought I could see trains running through the eyes of the homeless man muttering in front of the Hess station. Trains with snakes crawling though the fluorescent lights, making them flicker. Stephanie once told me she could see trains running through my eyes when my blood sugar had gotten dangerously low. Today was Gay Pride Day; the streets on the West Side all the way into Greenwich Village were like straws stopped up with beetles and noisy thumbtacks laughing and hollering at each other. Homosexuals also scared me, but I had a small affinity for them as well: they were the last of each of their lineages, the last Sullivan, the last Perez, the last Hammann, the last of Britain's Wuensch dynasty.

We kept walking, and none of the people passing would look at us. I was so tired and hot I thought the buildings looked like swaying mountains of jello. "There's a starlet for you," Stephanie teased as a tanktop full of breasts went by. I didn't know if the tanktop had a head attached, but I didn't want to spend time dwelling on it. As it was I saw the city as a greenhouse of articulate ferns and chrysanthemums that spent most of their hours just holding the blood inside their frazzled wilting bodies.

Presidents Day

The snow sleeping in garbage cans
outside the walk-up tenement.

A man untangles the Christmas lights
from his fire escape.

The flag chewed to its original blood color.

The city is quiet today.
The traffic signals have stopped
their insect-clicking,
just a menu slipped under the door

announcing peace for the new century,
and the delicious toxins offered
at the prices of old rain.

The sun climbs out from underneath
a nickel dead on the sidewalk.

The trees are weak, they have leukemia,
each branch bare and twitching in the wind,
shading the rats awake under day-old cement.

Ten spinach leaves fall out of a backpack.
On closer inspection they are human entrails,
but nobody looks at the ground.

Not the woman comforting a cigarette.
Not the doll that's been struck by a child.
Not the two lovers gazing into each other's cell phones.

Not the cold that makes each building seem like someone else's thoughts.

And then a man gets out of his cab,
and like someone who exists for only an hour,
removes his eyes and mutters
that there will be no more
suffering once the afternoon glare is gone,

once the dog he ran over darkens the sky
from where she shivers
in the basement of a stray coupon flyer

and the four-year-old disappearing on her stoop
eats her already bruised-open hand to keep it from making another sound.

Fascist Silence and a Sepia Democracy

Seven streets lined with black hole shops.
Seven taxi hideouts.
Seven streetlamps orbited by warplanes.

And today,
the shooting down of mosquitoes for fuel.

Seven stars in the sky.
Seven lights left on the ground.
Seven books that did not evaporate.

And today, the warplanes.

And tomorrow, the warplanes.

Seven from the wall of a tenement
warmed with someone's bowels,

the silence and democracy of that man
during a future autumn,

his own blood and that of the mosquitoes
who interrogated him
by picking his eyes from the unfinished light,

not eyes, but holes where he's hidden everything.

And then the autumn remembered only by cameras
while they fade into blemishes,

at least one leaf that falls and destroys a city

where curtains who've lost their souls
drift endlessly
inside a mourning dove

and where seven trees make the sound of seven skies approaching.

Gods That are Noticed Only When They Stop Watching Us

A stack of books—a building with no windows,

and someone outside cooking his body
over the fires of obsolete
police blotters.

Someone searching for adolescence—
the bands that vanished inside your stereo.

*

The open-mic poet trying
not to disturb what he's written.

His audience keeps disappearing and returning,
maybe with one less eyelash,

another color between darkness and blackout.

*

Only one call this autumn—
the phone picking up echoes
of prairies-ago Canada geese.
The house you started from

a reminder of someone's gossip.
The house itself

inexpensive, left behind
by starlings.

*

Spring snow:
all the heartbeats you've lost,

the slums omitted
from a Pennsylvania twilight map,
the death of an iris.

"The world is finished, but in some other
rainfall," you said
from the newspaper's hinges,
the beginning of drought season.

*

A man selling the next night,
five dollars, preparation
for yet another
grocery closing down.

The sky kept above them by the names they've chosen.

*

The word *fuck* and the blaring way
it does not forgive you.

People live there,
drinking and working and celebrating.

Long-distance trucks passing with their eyes boarded up.

Trees that sleep in the neighborhood
and trees too tired to hold any longer
the birds that help them breathe.

*

One town is called
Last Year's Child Abuse Convictions, Population: Many.

Another, I Hate You, Population: All,
and the next, Eat Shit And Die, Population: Evan Blumb.

*

A human ravaged by his honest physique
having dinner with light left in the mirror:
face like a crop failure, a furrow of warlocks,

wind blowing the eyes somewhere,

the threat of rain inside the blurred reflection.

A haiku survivor counting shadow blossoms
from a house at the far end
of the moonlight.

The sky dragged away
by pheasants.

The space between stars, also, is gone.

THE INSIDE OF THE BODY IS NOT RED
BUT DARK LIKE A POLITICAL IDEOLOGY

1.

A box of mountains
and tree smoke arrives by truck.

The Game of Appalachia:

three teenagers sculpting with chainsaws
behind the fumes
of the mini-mart,

a man with no belt to hold him
spitting strands and streams
of Copenhagen.

No police trail of red screams.

Only his fingerprints,
the dollar he touched
and the presidents betrayed there.

Identity theft
committed by the parking lot
still wet with skunk.

2.

The cashier harasses a drivers license
from the gray-haired man and his limping cane
when he requests a pack
of Marlboro Ultra Lites,

each waiting for the other to break,

each not quite a trap gone empty or missing,

the weight of the Exxon light
still fresh on their backs.

3.

A boy scraped dry
and forced into the restroom stall
with a handful of deer feces,

what the professors who crouch
in the woods call
animal static,

a boy scraped dry
to write with animal static
the Collected Goodwill of Ann Coulter:

it will never keep anyone awake,

the killing of so many
words,

the six hundred opinions
counted and corrected today,
the six hundred daughters
of Sasquatch counted,
but not corrected, so far.

4.

The deer will not be fed.
The brook trout will no longer follow
water to more fatal water.

It is not safe to say, "Goodnight."

Money ends where the creek bed ends.

The tiredness of all money
south of a mine collapse.

"We go to the mini-mart where diabetes grows."

Folks read to their flesh
with the same name
(and the same name over again)
from the cigarette-thin bibles.

And nothing gets to claim
it's been abolished
during that undiagnosed insomnia,

the lifetime of a man eroded
to nothing but blood sugar whiskey

and black lung mountain views.

REPUBLICAN BROADCASTS

A fog of mountains
and bird shrouds
arrives at least one chicken cry
ahead of the light.

A man injured
from a too-short sleep
revives last night's coffee
in his blinking, nuclear oven.

His companion complains
of a noise in her
head,

but not the morning programs
and their right-to-live
pornography.

A breeze's duration of deer
drifts into the yard,

their silence prohibited.

The man says nothing
to his companion,
but in a greeting card accent,
like Geraldo Rivera,

like cancer,

*a punishment
for the silences of the body.*

The deer vanish behind a wound in the fog.

The woman corrects her face
with a frown of lipstick:
"Look where the animals are eating the mist."

And near the disappearing bus stop,

children throwing stones
at a tree that doesn't belong there.

Morris & Essex Line, Blackout

At the arriving station nothing exits
but a cell phone couple, and the man

with eyes boiled shut and a gash
on his forehead muttering for god to give him

a happy life and valuable skills,

ten minutes of gentle cursing where I am
too late to find

how many lights began
across the Hudson, how many cars

across the glisten of deershine,

the train that is a trail of horses,
the train that sniffs out platforms in the dusk

Tonight the city's cancelled
go back to where you started
no power in the northeast

I gather my things that are more humid today
a hole in the schedule the terrorists found--

Arrival, eight-thirty-three, Dover,

railyards passing and the sky
buried for six miles ahead,

conductors planting rows of tickets in the blackening east.

Midtown direct, To the Ends of New Jersey

following locust tracks
across the sun,

the last train

coming from Hoboken,
Morris Plains,
Denville

trees running
against the train through

rusted yards of lightning

a man holding a snail to his ear
outside Belle & Blade War Video

house by the Dover station
a garden lit with petals of crossing lights

next stop for employees only
do not leave the car
do not get up with your bags

do not change seats or move

a man waking
beneath a newspaper

tells me I have eyes

clotted with signals
from an earlier train

how did you make it
this far, he asks
taking a sip of carbonated sunlight

and flagging down the only conductor

the towns written on his
wrists and spreading with every
kind of gaze

the hard-moving
windows, their blurred townships

and trees from a different hour

how many stops now until dusk
how many stops until the newspapers
left behind on the seats
help each other

and the afternoon where my ticket—
dug up with graves
of smaller minutes
belonging to smaller towns—

ends in someone else's hands

do not leave your shoes
asleep where they're sitting

do not stand between cars

it is no longer safe to speak
or stand anywhere

announcement: tomorrow we will have
no room for voices
tomorrow leave your voice at home

but right now the day is on schedule

right now Mickey and Kathy Kristoff
wait for the wrong matchbox car
the one without miles or radio moods
in Great Meadows, 1973

once again, do not stand

do not hide your intentions beneath a cough

do not reveal by turning the nervous pages
of a schedule that the train is going
to run out of light

do not let the book you're reading
exaggerate any winters
even if the first page loses Hopatcong
and Mount Olive
with a frown's hurried silence

do not scrawl the seat with your
5:30 pm eyes and fingers

the place you're sitting is already
an exact population
of go-away's and goodbye's

and though we are closer
to the towns where trees go
home safely at night

do not ask how many stations

how many stations
huddled among the caffeine checkpoints
and pizza dens
and Shop Rite Liquor puddles
before we know each other

as the evenings of Hackettstown again

The Dirtbag on Election Day

Because I am smaller
than the newspaper today

I can vote only
for the shadows who've gathered

on my wall to kill themselves.

Two men the size of nails
hide under a sheet torn from a notebook

where I've spelled their mouths wrong

and erased all of their skin.

I glue them back together with bread
that I've already chewed
and spit out.

It is always Tuesday.
Five years without work or sleep
or anyone who remembers Monday's final collapse.

My thoughts now spider missions
between cracks in the floor,

I've run out of safe places
to hide from the two presidents
on television flickering and destroying each other.

I worry about waking up with nothing
around me but the chasms
of former dirtbags:

Ronald Heaven, Chris Bludgeon,
Wells Fargo, the thirty-five CEOs
named Jim Frank who shoveled herpes
for *Perverted Sunset.*

So I stay up until morning and bludgeon,
for them, my best song,
my one entrail,

ways to arouse the unpublishable near-women
filing their nails on the other end
of 900 numbers,

and how to seduce them with our backward
swastikas, our backward and obsolete swastikas.

Scene from the Han-Kahan

Today a deli clerk sniffed
the polio in my January fur.

I was thirsty and holding
a bottle of vaccine

mixed with diet A&W.
The clerk smiled with her

precise and tender teeth
and took her eyes out

right in front of me,
dropped them softly on the counter.

Two bullets where I should've
seen some kind of retinal blood.

Two bullets that she scooped
out of her head and put in her mouth,

washing them down with cockroach salt.
Then she put her eyes back

and there was nothing left,
nothing at all in the world,

and I could smell the soldiers
at her mouth-edge,

the ends of her language,
the way she curled up

like a hookworm in her own
brown hands.

we're certain there are places in the Oklahoma night where it was never America. we're certain there are bombs blooming in the haunches of grass that sweat from holding onto September, and i'm certain of this, too: i'm certain to continue tracking flycatchers across the fast-moving sky, and find the cloud that taught my father how to learn from his own speaking, and the storm sculptures who slept with my mother, telling her nobody ever stood straighter than she, or moved more loneliness out of Wisconsin, Minnesota, Michigan. we better have mosquitoes we can grind into wheat that lasts a decade, because i'm certain of the terror of Elk City and the terror of Weatherford, and i'm certain of my administration. there's kids maturing into screen savers, and there's vanishing, and there's microbes, and flowers who want to scar each other. and we have madmen scrawled on our overpasses: *Trenchcoats Rule; Welcome to Iraq, Kansas; It'll take time to restore the chaos; 9/11 Yes!* i'm certain that the redbuds will go on hurting right where the sparrows have marked up the air with smiles. and i'm certain that we'll wake with enough land for a mailbox and a bit of walking and enough water to wash our tongues, but only once. i'm certain there are farms where children can go on for days petting our corn. and though i'm certain we have many Icelands loping through the fields and leading away our winter, the peace we dug up in the dim Tulsa satellites will be maintained.

THE HERMIT KINGDOM

we pray the starving who are still
far from becoming wind will not pick up our scent.

we want mornings without fear
of the coming light,

without having only bones to eat.

we want succor between silhouettes,
picnics on the bank of the strangled river,

trips to the museum with nothing
in it but a family of four hired to keep their eyes
focused on the exhibits of bare walls and corners.

we want expeditions to the park
where weeds gasp under the groping radiation,

and to ride the Ferris wheel that never turns.

we want enough food to sleep safely
and for the ice wind to stop
scraping away our hands
and the paintings of where we lived.

we want the satellites to stay in the sky
at night because they are the only
lights, the only signs of warmth anywhere.

we want to share our days and our interpretation
of days and the black market photos
of our president nursing his hermit genitalia.

we want a Chinese soldier, someone
to hold onto to grasp for over our texts

about the abomination of the individual

while windflower shadows pick us off
one at a time starting

from the solitary light bulb burning
for ten minutes among the cave towers
at the edge of our city

where the ground's been turned away
and we can no longer find our tunnels

and where we hear rats ticking and scratching
through the bowels of the frozen sky.

Rob Cook lives in New York City's East Village. He is the author of six collections, including *Blueprints for a Genocide* (Spuyten Duyvil, 2012), *Empire in the Shade of a Grass Blade* (Bitter Oleander Press, 2013) and *Asking My Liver for Forgiveness* (Rain Mountain Press, 2014). Work has appeared in *Asheville Poetry Review, Caliban, Fence, A cappella Zoo, Zoland Poetry, Tampa Review, Minnesota Review, Aufgabe, Caketrain, Many Mountains Moving, Hampden-Sydney Poetry Review, Harvard Review, Colorado Review, Bomb (online), Sugar House Review, Mudfish, Pleiades, Versal, Weave, Wisconsin Review, Ur Vox, Heavy Feather Review, Phantom Drift, Osiris,* etc.

34270746R00084

Made in the USA
Charleston, SC
04 October 2014